Table of Contents

Super-Fast Turtleback,
page 6

Turtleback Bed Jacket,
page 18

Double Lace Turtleback,
page 12

Turtleback Jacket,
page 8

Introduction

Who would believe you could make a jacket from a rectangle?

A few years ago, we saw a garment called a "turtleback" in a catalog. At the time, we were fascinated with the title and tucked the picture away. Recently, we ran across this picture and decided that it would be neat to see if we could crochet or knit such a garment. When we set about figuring out how to make such a piece, we discovered—to our surprise—that it was just a rectangle. You stitch a rectangle, then fold and sew it to make the shape come alive.

Rib patterns seem to be the key to a good fit. Having a soft, pliable yarn is another must. We have a sample in our shop, and everyone who tries it on loves the effect. We believe this "pop-on" garment will become a favorite for knitters of all skill levels and ages. You just pop it on and wear it as fitted and cuddly, or loose and flowing as you want. Enjoy!

Meet The Designers

Sue Childress

I was born in a very small town to a mother who loved crafts and crochet. I've been married to Robert since 1957. We have two children and five grandchildren.

When my children were small, I would ask them if they liked what I was making. If they said no, then I would never make that item again. When my sister Frances and I were attending craft fairs, my daughter was a good gauge for us. If she liked a project, it was always a best-seller.

My sister and I opened Stitches 'N Stuff Yarn and Gift Shop in 1984. I have enjoyed being a part of the yarn industry with all its ups and downs. I never get tired of all the wonderful yarns and notions that have flooded our world over the last few years.

I've known how to crochet since I was a little girl, but I didn't learn to knit until I was 54. I've enjoyed knitting as much as crocheting. It's much more fun to know how to do both!

Frances Hughes

I was born in a small town in East Texas, and I am 75 years young. My husband and I have been married since 1952. We have two sons, nine adult grandchildren and eight great-grandchildren.

I learned to crochet at a very young age. Being left-handed made this a challenge, but the rewards far outweighed the effort it took. Then, much later in life, I learned to knit. Knitting opened up a whole new way of expressing myself through my needlecrafting, broadening my horizons.

My sister Sue and I opened a yarn shop in 1984. It has been plenty of fun and quite a bit of work, but I love it all. I sold my first design to Annie's Attic in 1984 after telling Sue that if she could do that, I could too.

Sue and I have had designs published by Annie's Attic, Needlecraft Shop, House of White Birches and Leisure Arts. My designs have also been in several magazines, including *Knitting Digest, Creative Knitting, Crochet World, Old-Time Crochet, McCalls, Country Woman* and *Ribbon Works*.

Folding & Wearing Turtleback Jackets

1. Once you have your rectangle/square knitted, fold it in half widthwise. Sew the two edges together as indicated on the pattern and in the photo, leaving an open area for your arms.

2. This garment is very flexible because of the ribbing pattern. With one hand placed along the front top edge, lift the top half of the garment. Slip the other arm through one of the armholes.

3. Slip the other arm into the second armhole.

4. Pull the garment around you, making it as form-fitting or as loose as you prefer. If you want a collar, turn back the edge around your neck.

House of White Birches, Berne, Indiana 46711   DRGnetwork.com

Royal Rib Turtleback

Design by Frances Hughes

Skill Level

 ■■□□ EASY

Sizes

Woman's small (medium, large, extra-large)
Instructions are given for smallest size, with larger
sizes in parentheses. When only 1 number is given it
applies to all sizes.

Finished Measurements

Approx 36 (38, 40, 42) inches square, before folding

Materials

- S.R. Kertzer Marble Chunky (bulky weight
  yarn; 100% acrylic; 341 yds/200g per ball):
  2 (2, 3, 3) balls majesty #15
- Size 10½ (6.5mm) 29-inch circular needle
- Size 17 (12mm) 29-inch circular needle
- Tapestry needle

5 BULKY

Gauge

12 sts = 4 inches/10cm on smaller needle in pat.
Exact gauge is not critical to project.

Special Abbreviation

Cross-stitch (X-st): K3, pass 3rd st on RH needle over
first 2 sts and off needle.

Pattern Notes

Piece is worked as a square,
and then folded and sewn at
the sides, leaving openings
for the armholes. When
worn, the looseness of the rib
pattern tends to cause the
piece to "grow" in width for
a flexible fit.

When measuring the length
of the piece, be sure to do
so with the piece on a
flat surface.

Instructions

With larger needle, loosely
cast on 103 (113, 123, 133) sts.

Row 1 (WS): K1, p1-tbl, k1, *p2, k1, p1-tbl, k1; rep
from * across.

Row 2 (RS): P1, k1-tbl, p1, *k1, yo, k1, p1, k1-tbl, p1;
rep from * across—123 (135, 147, 159) sts.

Row 3: K1, p1-tbl, k1, *p3, k1, p1-tbl, k1; rep
from * across.

Row 4: P1, k1-tbl, p1, *X-st, p1, k1-tbl, p1; rep from *
across—103 (113, 123, 133) sts.

Rep [Rows 1–4] twice.

Change to smaller needle and continue working
Rows 1–4 of pat until piece measures 31 (33, 35, 37)
inches from cast-on edge.

Change to larger needle and work [Rows 1–4]
3 times.

Bind off loosely.

Finishing

Referring to diagram, fold piece in half matching
cast-on and bound-off larger-needle edges.
Mark sides 7½ (8, 8½, 9) inches from fold for arm
openings. Sew side seams tog joining area 3 to area
2 and area 4 to area 1 from marker to lower edge.

When worn, 1 large-needle end becomes the collar
and the other becomes the flounce. ❖

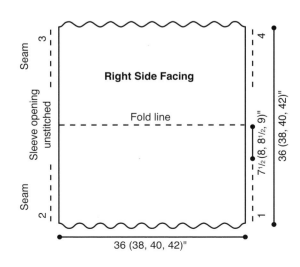

Super-Fast Turtleback

Design by Sue Childress

Skill Level

 EASY

Sizes

Woman's small (medium, large, extra-large)
Instructions are given for smallest size, with larger sizes in parentheses. When only 1 number is given it applies to all sizes.

Finished Measurements

Approx 28 x 32 (30 x 34, 32 x 36, 34 x 38) inches, before folding

Materials

- Araucania Limari (bulky weight yarn; 70% merino wool/20% alpaca/10% silk; 73 yds/100g per hank): 6 (7, 8, 9) hanks turquoise/blue variegated #554
- Size 13 (9mm) 29-inch circular needle
- Size 17 (12mm) 29-inch circular needle
- Tapestry needle

Gauge

11 sts = 4 inches/10cm on smaller needle in pat. Exact gauge is not critical to this project.

Pattern Stitch

Feather Rib (multiple of 5 sts + 2)

Row 1 (RS): P2, *yo, k2tog-tbl, k1, p2; rep from * across.

Row 2: K2, *yo, k2tog-tbl, p1, k2; rep from * across.

Pattern Notes

Piece is worked as a rectangle, and then folded and sewn at the sides, leaving openings for the armholes. When worn, the looseness of the rib pattern tends to cause the piece to "grow" in width for a flexible fit.

When measuring the length of the piece, be sure to do so with the piece on a flat surface.

Instructions

With larger needle, loosely cast on 92 (97, 102, 107) sts.

Rep [Rows 1 and 2 of Feather Rib pat] 10 times.

Change to smaller needle and continue working Rows 1 and 2 of pat until piece measures 22 (24, 26, 28) inches from cast-on edge, ending by working Row 2 of pat.

Change to larger needle and work [Rows 1 and 2 of pat] 10 times.

Bind off loosely.

Finishing

Referring to diagram, fold piece in half matching cast-on and bound-off larger-needle edges. Mark sides 7½ (8, 8½, 9) inches from fold for arm openings. Sew side seams tog joining area 3 to area 2 and area 4 to area 1 from marker to lower edge.

When worn, 1 large-needle end becomes the collar and the other becomes the flounce. ❖

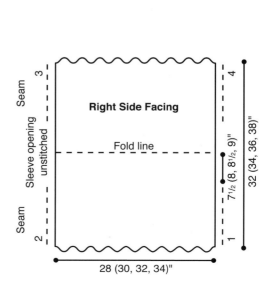

Right Side Facing

Fold line

Seam 3

Sleeve opening unstitched

Seam 2

7½ (8, 8½, 9)"

32 (34, 36, 38)"

28 (30, 32, 34)"

Turtleback Jacket

Design by Sue Childress

Skill Level
 EASY

Sizes
Woman's small (medium, large, extra-large) Instructions are given for smallest size, with larger sizes in parentheses. When only 1 number is given it applies to all sizes.

Finished Measurements
Approx 32 x 40 (34 x 42, 36 x 44, 38 x 46) inches, before folding

Materials
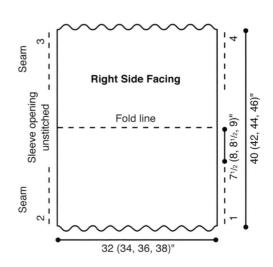

- Araucania Azapa (bulky weight yarn; 45% merino wool/30% alpaca/15% silk/10% Donegal wool; 198 yds/100g per hank): 5 (6, 7, 8) hanks tan #802
- Size 10½ (6.5mm) 29-inch circular needle
- Size 17 (12mm) 29-inch circular needle
- Tapestry needle

Gauge
12 sts = 4 inches/10cm on smaller needle in St st. Exact gauge is not critical to this project.

Pattern Stitch
Eyelet & Slip Stitch Rib (multiple of 11 sts + 7)

Row 1 (RS): P3, sl 1k wyib, p3, *k1, yo, k2tog, k1, p3, sl 1k wyib, p3; rep from * across.

Row 2: K3, p1, k3, *p4, k3, p1, k3; rep from * across.

Row 3: P3, sl 1k wyib, p3, *k1, ssk, yo, k1, p3, sl 1k wyib, p3; rep from * across.

Row 4: Rep Row 2.

Rep Rows 1–4 for pat.

Pattern Notes
Piece is worked as a rectangle, and then folded and sewn at the sides, leaving openings for the armholes. When worn, the looseness of the rib pattern tends to cause the piece to "grow" in width for a flexible fit.

When measuring the length of the piece, be sure to do so with the piece on a flat surface.

Instructions
With larger needle, loosely cast on 117 (128, 139, 150) sts.

Rep [Rows 1–4 of Eyelet & Slip St Rib pat] 6 times.

Change to smaller needle and continue working Rows 1–4 of pat until piece measures 32 (34, 36, 38) inches from cast-on edge, ending by working a Row 4 of pat.

Change to larger needle and work [Rows 1–4] 6 times.

Bind off loosely.

Finishing
Referring to diagram, fold piece in half matching cast-on and bound-off larger-needle edges. Mark sides 7½ (8, 8½, 9) inches from fold for arm openings. Sew side seams tog joining area 3 to area 2 and area 4 to area 1 from marker to lower edge.

When worn, 1 large-needle end becomes the collar and the other becomes the flounce. ❖

Right Side Facing

Fold line

Seam 3

Sleeve opening unstitched

Seam 2

Seam 4

7½ (8, 8½, 9)"

40 (42, 44, 46)"

1

32 (34, 36, 38)"

Grande Red Turtleback

Design by Sue Childress

Skill Level

 EASY

Sizes

Woman's small (medium, large, extra-large) Instructions are given for smallest size, with larger sizes in parentheses. When only 1 number is given it applies to all sizes.

Finished Measurements

Approx 32 x 38 (34 x 40, 36 x 42, 38 x 44) inches, before folding

Materials

- Plymouth Baby Alpaca Grande (bulky weight yarn; 100% baby alpaca; 110 yds/ 100g per skein): 6 (7, 8, 9) skeins red #2050
- Size 10½ (6.5mm) 29-inch circular needle
- Size 17 (12mm) 29-inch circular needle
- Tapestry needle

5 BULKY

Gauge

12 sts = 4 inches/10cm on smaller needle in pat. Exact gauge is not critical to this project.

Pattern Stitch

Pique Rib (multiple of 10 sts + 3)

Row 1 (RS): K3, *p3, k1, p3, k3; rep from * across.

Row 2: P3, *k3, p1, k3, p3; rep from * across.

Row 3: Rep Row 1.

Row 4: Knit.

Rep Rows 1–4 for pat.

Pattern Notes

Piece is worked as a rectangle, and then folded and sewn at the sides, leaving openings for the armholes. When worn, the looseness of the rib pattern tends to cause the piece to "grow" in width for a flexible fit.

When measuring the length of the piece, be sure to do so with the piece on a flat surface.

Instructions

With larger needle, loosely cast on 103 (113, 123, 133) sts.

Rep [Rows 1–4 of Pique Rib pat] 3 times.

Change to smaller needle and continue working Rows 1–4 of pat until piece measures 32 (34, 36, 38) inches from cast-on edge, ending by working Row 4 of pat.

Change to larger needle and work [Rows 1–4] 3 times.

Bind off loosely.

Finishing

Referring to diagram, fold piece in half matching cast-on and bound-off larger-needle edges. Mark sides 7½ (8, 8½, 9) inches from fold for arm openings. Sew side seams tog joining area 3 to area 2 and area 4 to area 1 from marker to lower edge.

When worn, 1 large-needle end becomes the collar and the other becomes the flounce. ❖

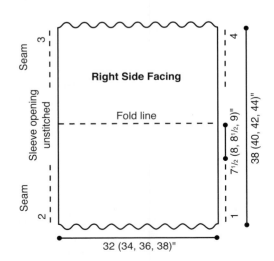

Right Side Facing

Fold line

Seam 3

Sleeve opening unstitched

Seam 2

4

7½ (8, 8½, 9)"

1

38 (40, 42, 44)"

32 (34, 36, 38)"

Double Lace Turtleback

Design by Frances Hughes

Skill Level

 EASY

Sizes

Woman's small (medium, large, extra-large)
Instructions are given for smallest size, with larger sizes in parentheses. When only 1 number is given it applies to all sizes.

Finished Measurements

Approx 32 x 38 (34 x 40, 36 x 42, 38 x 44) inches, before folding

Materials

- Sirdar Click Chunky (bulky weight yarn; 70% acrylic/30% wool; 81 yds/50g per ball): 9 (10, 11, 12) balls cranberry #130
- Size 10½ (6.5mm) 29-inch circular needle
- Size 17 (12mm) 29-inch circular needle
- Tapestry needle

Gauge

16 sts = 4 inches/10cm on smaller needle in St st. Exact gauge is not critical to this project.

Pattern Stitch

Double Lace Rib (multiple 6 sts + 2)

Row 1 (RS): K2, *p1, yo, k2tog-tbl, p1, k2; rep from * across.

Row 2: P2, *k1, p2; rep from * across.

Row 3: K2, *p1, k2tog, yo, p1, k2; rep from * across.

Row 4: Rep Row 2.

Rep Rows 1–4 for pat.

Pattern Notes

Piece is worked as a rectangle, and then folded and sewn at the sides, leaving openings for the armholes. When worn, the looseness of the rib pattern tends to cause the piece to "grow" in width for a flexible fit.

When measuring the length of the piece, be sure to do so with the piece on a flat surface.

Instructions

With larger needle, loosely cast on 110 (122, 134, 146) sts.

Rep [Rows 1–4 of Double Lace Rib pat] 3 times.

Change to smaller needle and continue working Rows 1–4 of pat until piece measures about 33 (35, 37, 39) inches from cast-on edge, ending by working Row 4 of pat.

Change to larger needle and work [Rows 1–4] 3 times.

Bind off loosely.

Finishing

Referring to diagram, fold piece in half matching cast-on and bound-off larger-needle edges. Mark sides 7½ (8, 8½, 9) inches from fold for arm openings. Sew side seams tog joining area 3 to area 2 and area 4 to area 1 from marker to lower edge.

When worn, 1 large-needle end becomes the collar and the other becomes the flounce. ❖

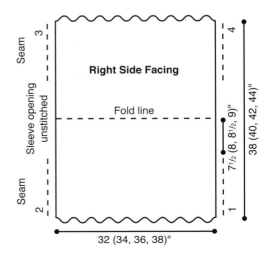

Turtleback on the Town

Design by Frances Hughes

Skill Level

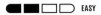 EASY

Sizes

Woman's small (medium, large, extra-large) Instructions are given for smallest size, with larger sizes in parentheses. When only 1 number is given it applies to all sizes.

Finished Measurements

Approx 32 x 38 (34 x 40, 36 x 42, 38 x 44) inches, before folding

Materials

- Katia Ingenua (medium weight yarn; 78% mohair/13% nylon/9% wool; 153 yds/50g per ball): 4 balls black #02
- Katia Gatsby (light weight yarn; 77% viscose/15% nylon/8% metallic polyester; 115 yds/50g): 5 balls black with gold #503
- Size 10½ (6.5mm) 29-inch circular needle
- Size 17 (12mm) 29-inch circular needle
- Tapestry needle

Gauge

14 sts = 4 inches/10cm in St st on smaller needle with 1 strand of each yarn held tog.
Exact gauge is not critical to this project.

Pattern Stitch

Perforated Rib (multiple of 6 sts + 3)

Row 1 (RS): P1, k1, p1, *yo, p3tog, yo, p1, k1, p1; rep from * across.

Row 2: K1, p1, k1, *p3, k1, p1, k1; rep from * across.

Row 3: P1, k1, p1, *k3, p1, k1, p1; rep from * across.

Row 4: Rep Row 2.

Rep Rows 1–4 for pat.

Pattern Notes

Piece is worked as a rectangle, and then folded and sewn at the sides, leaving openings for the armholes. When worn, the looseness of the rib pattern tends to cause the piece to "grow" in width for a flexible fit.

When measuring the length of the piece, be sure to do so with the piece on a flat surface.

Instructions

With larger needle and 1 strand of each yarn held tog, loosely cast on 99 (111, 123, 135) sts.

Rep [Rows 1–4 of Perforated Rib pat] 3 times.

Change to smaller needle and continue working Row 1–4 of pat until piece measures about 32 (34, 36, 38) inches from cast-on edge, ending by working Row 4 of pat.

Change to larger needle and rep [Rows 1–4] 3 times.

Bind off loosely.

Finishing

Referring to diagram, fold piece in half matching cast-on and bound-off larger-needle edges. Mark sides 7½ (8, 8½, 9) inches from fold for arm openings. Sew side seams tog joining area 3 to area 2 and area 4 to area 1 from marker to lower edge.

When worn, 1 large-needle end becomes the collar and the other becomes the flounce. ❖

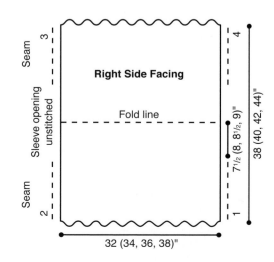

Baby Turtleback

Design by Frances Hughes

Skill Level

 EASY

Sizes

Infant's 0–6 (6–12, 12–18, 18–24) months
Instructions are given for smallest size, with larger sizes in parentheses. When only 1 number is given it applies to all sizes.

Finished Measurements

Approx 14 (16, 18, 20) inches square, before folding

Materials

- Sirdar Snuggly Baby Bamboo (light weight yarn; 80% bamboo/20% wool; 104 yds/50g per ball): 2 (2, 3, 3) balls coo #148
- Size 7 (4.5mm) 24-inch circular needle
- Size 10½ (6.5mm) 24-inch circular needle
- Tapestry needle
- ⅔ yard 1½ to 2½-inch-wide ribbon (optional for closure)

Gauge

13 sts = 4 inches/10cm in St st on smaller needle
Exact gauge is not critical to this project.

Pattern Stitch

Bluebell Rib (multiple of 5 sts + 2)

Row 1 (RS): P2, *k3, p2; rep from * across.

Rows 2 and 4: K2, *p3, k2; rep from * across.

Row 3: P2, *k3, p2; rep from * across.

Row 5: P2, *yo, sl 1, k2tog, psso, yo, p2; rep from * across.

Row 6: Rep Row 2.

Rep Rows 1–6 for pat.

Pattern Notes

Piece is worked as a square, and then folded and sewn at the sides, leaving openings for the armholes. When worn, the looseness of the rib pattern tends to cause the piece to "grow" in width for a flexible fit.

When measuring the length of the piece, be sure to do so with the piece on a flat surface.

Instructions

With larger needle, loosely cast on 82 (92, 102, 112) sts.

Rep [Rows 1–6 of Bluebell Rib pat] 1 (1, 2, 2) times.

Change to smaller needle and continue in pat until piece measures 12 (14, 16, 18) inches from cast-on edge, ending by working Row 6 of pat.

Change to larger needle and work [Rows 1–6] 2 (2, 3, 3) times.

Bind off loosely.

Finishing

Referring to diagram, fold piece in half matching cast-on and bound-off larger-needle edges. Mark sides 3 (3½, 4, 4½) inches from fold for armhole openings. Sew side seams tog joining area 3 to area 2 and area 4 to area 1 from marker to lower edge.

Referring to photo, weave ribbon between sts on each side and tie at center front.

When worn, 1 large-needle end becomes the collar and the other becomes the flounce. ❖

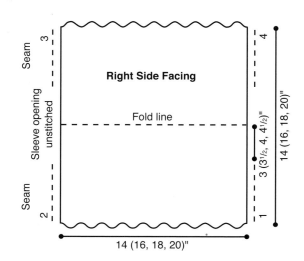

Turtleback Bed Jacket

Design by Sue Childress

Skill Level

 EASY

Sizes

Woman's extra-small (small, medium, large, extra-large) Instructions are given for smallest size, with larger sizes in parentheses. When only 1 number is given it applies to all sizes.

Finished Measurements

Approx 26 (28, 30, 32, 34) inches square, before folding

Materials

- Berroco Comfort (medium weight yarn; 50% super fine nylon/50% super fine acrylic; 210 yds/100g per ball): 3 (3, 4, 4, 5) balls ivory #9701
- Size 9 (5.5mm) 29-inch circular needle or size needed to obtain gauge
- Size 13 (9mm) 29-inch circular needle
- Tapestry needle
- ¾ yard ¼-inch-wide matching ribbon (optional for closure)

Gauge

16 sts and 16 rows = 4 inches/10cm on smaller needle in pat.
Exact gauge is not critical to this project.

Special Abbreviation

Slip, knit, pass (skp): Sl next st, k1, pass slipped st over knit st.

Pattern Stitch

Open Chain Rib (multiple of 6 sts + 2)

Row 1 (WS): K2, *p4, k2; rep from * across.

Row 2 (RS): P2, *k2tog, [yo] twice, skp, p2; rep from * across.

Row 3: K2, *p1, purl in front of first loop and in back of 2nd loop of double yo, p1, k2; rep from * across.

Row 4: P2, *yo, skp, k2tog, yo, p2; rep from * across.

Rep Rows 1–4 for pat.

Pattern Notes

Piece is worked as a square, and then folded and sewn at the sides, leaving openings for the armholes. When worn, the looseness of the rib pattern tends to cause the piece to "grow" in width for a flexible fit.

When measuring the length of the piece, be sure to do so with the piece on a flat surface.

Instructions

With larger needle, loosely cast on 128 (134, 140, 146, 152) sts.

Rep [Rows 1–4 of Open Chain Rib pat] 5 times.

Change to smaller needle and continue working Rows 1–4 of pat until piece measures 21 (23, 25, 27, 29) inches from cast-on edge, ending by working a Row 4.

Change to larger needle and work [Rows 1–4] 5 times.

Bind off loosely.

Finishing

Referring to diagram, fold piece in half matching cast-on and bound-off larger-needle edges. Mark sides 7 (7½, 8, 8½, 9) inches from fold for arm openings. Sew side seams tog joining area 3 to area 2 and area 4 to area 1 from marker to lower edge.

Referring to photo, weave ribbon between sts on each side and tie at center front, if ribbon closure is desired.

When worn, 1 large-needle end becomes the collar and the other becomes the flounce. ❖

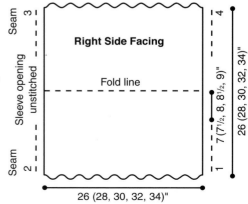

Knitting Basics

Cast On

Leaving an end about an inch long for each stitch to be cast on, make a slip knot on the right needle.

Place the thumb and index finger of your left hand between the yarn ends with the long yarn end over your thumb, and the strand from the skein over your index finger. Close your other fingers over the strands to hold them against your palm. Spread your thumb and index fingers apart and draw the yarn into a "V."

Place the needle in front of the strand around your thumb and bring it underneath this strand. Carry the needle over and under the strand on your index finger.

Draw through loop on thumb.

Drop the loop from your thumb and draw up the strand to form a stitch on the needle.

Repeat until you have cast on the number of stitches indicated in the pattern. Remember to count the beginning slip knot as a stitch.

Cable Cast On

This type of cast-on is used when adding stitches in the middle or at the end of a row.

Make a slip knot on the left needle. Knit a stitch in this knot and place it on the left needle. Insert the right needle between the last two stitches on the left needle. Knit a stitch and place it on the left needle. Repeat for each stitch needed.

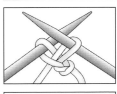

Knit (k)

Insert tip of right needle from front to back in next stitch on left needle.

Bring yarn under and over the tip of the right needle.

Pull yarn loop through the stitch with right needle point.

Slide the stitch off the left needle. The new stitch is on the right needle.

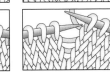

Purl (p)

With yarn in front, insert tip of right needle from back to front through next stitch on the left needle. Bring yarn around the right needle counterclockwise. With right needle, draw yarn back through the stitch.

Slide the stitch off the left needle. The new stitch is on the right needle.

Bind Off

Binding off (knit)

Knit first two stitches on left needle. Insert tip of left needle into first stitch worked on right needle and pull it over the second stitch and completely off the needle.

Knit the next stitch and repeat. When one stitch remains on right needle, cut yarn and draw tail through last stitch to fasten off.

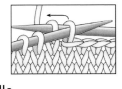

Binding off (purl)

Purl first two stitches on left needle. Insert tip of left needle into first stitch worked on right needle and pull it over the second stitch and completely off the needle.

Purl the next stitch and repeat. When one stitch remains on right needle, cut yarn and draw tail through last stitch to fasten off.

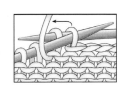

Increase (inc)

Two stitches in one stitch

Increase (knit)
Knit the next stitch in the usual manner, but don't remove the stitch from the left needle. Place right needle behind left needle and knit again into the back of the same stitch. Slip original stitch off left needle.

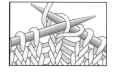

Increase (purl)
Purl the next stitch in the usual manner, but don't remove the stitch from the left needle. Place right needle behind left needle and purl again into the back of the same stitch. Slip original stitch off left needle.

Invisible Increase (M1)
There are several ways to make or increase one stitch.

Make 1 with Left Twist (M1L)
Insert left needle from front to back under the horizontal loop between the last stitch worked and next stitch on left needle.

   With right needle, knit into the back of this loop.

   To make this increase on the purl side, insert left needle in same manner and purl into the back of the loop.

Make 1 with Right Twist (M1R)
Insert left needle from back to front under the horizontal loop between the last stitch worked and next stitch on left needle.

   With right needle, knit into the front of this loop.

   To make this increase on the purl side, insert left needle in same manner and purl into the front of the loop.

Make 1 with Backward Loop over the right needle
With your thumb, make a loop over the right needle.
Slip the loop from your thumb onto the needle and pull to tighten.

Make 1 in top of stitch below
Insert tip of right needle into the stitch on left needle one row below.

   Knit this stitch, then knit the stitch on the left needle.

Decrease (dec)

Knit 2 together (k2tog)
Put tip of right needle through next two stitches on left needle as to knit. Knit these two stitches as one.

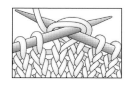

Purl 2 together (p2tog)
Put tip of right needle through next two stitches on left needle as to purl. Purl these two stitches as one.

Slip, Slip, Knit (ssk)
Slip next two stitches, one at a time, as to knit from left needle to right needle.

   Insert left needle in front of both stitches and work off needle together.

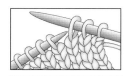
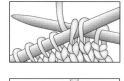

Slip, Slip, Purl (ssp)
Slip next two stitches, one at a time, as to knit from left needle to right needle. Slip these stitches back onto left needle keeping them twisted. Purl these two stitches together through back loops.

Standard Abbreviations

[ ] work instructions within brackets as many times as directed

( ) work instructions within parentheses in the place directed

** repeat instructions following the asterisks as directed

* repeat instructions following the single asterisk as directed

" inch(es)

approx approximately

beg begin/begins/beginning

CC contrasting color

ch chain stitch

cm centimeter(s)

cn cable needle

dec decrease/decreases/decreasing

dpn(s) double-point needle(s)

g gram(s)

inc increase/increases/increasing

k knit

k2tog knit 2 stitches together

kwise knitwise

LH left hand

m meter(s)

M1 make one stitch

MC main color

mm millimeter(s)

oz ounce(s)

p purl

pat(s) pattern(s)

p2tog purl 2 stitches together

psso pass slipped stitch over

p2sso pass 2 slipped stitches over

pwise purlwise

rem remain/remains/remaining

rep repeat(s)

rev St st reverse stockinette stitch

RH right hand

rnd(s) round(s)

RS right side

skp slip, knit, pass stitch over—one stitch decreased

sk2p slip 1, knit 2 together, pass slip stitch over the knit 2 together —2 stitches have been decreased

sl slip

sl 1k slip 1 knitwise

sl 1p slip 1 purlwise

sl st slip stitch(es)

ssk slip, slip, knit these 2 stitches together —a decrease

st(s) stitch(es)

St st stockinette stitch/ stocking stitch

tbl through back loop(s)

tog together

WS wrong side

wyib with yarn in back

wyif with yarn in front

yd(s) yard(s)

yfwd yarn forward

yo yarn over

Standard Yarn Weight System

Categories of yarn, gauge ranges, and recommended needle sizes

Yarn Weight Symbol & Category Names	1 SUPER FINE	2 FINE	3 LIGHT	4 MEDIUM	5 BULKY	6 SUPER BULKY
Type of Yarns in Category	Sock, Fingering, Baby	Sport, Baby	DK, Light Worsted	Worsted, Afghan, Aran	Chunky, Craft, Rug	Super Chunky, Roving
Knit Gauge Range* in Stockinette Stitch to 4 inches	27–32 sts	23–26 sts	21–24 sts	16–20 sts	12–15 sts	6–11 sts
Recommended Needle in Metric Size Range	2.25–3.25mm	3.25–3.75mm	3.75–4.5mm	4.5–5.5mm	5.5–8mm	8mm and larger
Recommended Needle U.S. Size Range	1 to 3	3 to 5	5 to 7	7 to 9	9 to 11	11 and larger

* GUIDELINES ONLY: The above reflect the most commonly used gauges and needle sizes for specific yarn categories.

Knitting Needle Conversion Chart

U.S.	1	2	3	4	5	6	7	8	9	10	10½	11	13	15	17	19	35	50
Continental-mm	2.25	2.75	3.25	3.5	3.75	4	4.5	5	5.5	6	6.5	8	9	10	12	15	19	25

Inches into Millimetres & Centimetres

All measurements are rounded off slightly.

inches	mm	cm	inches	cm	inches	cm	inches	cm	inches	cm
⅛	3	0.3	3	7.5	13	33.0	26	66.0	39	99.0
¼	6	0.6	3½	9.0	14	35.5	27	68.5	40	101.5
⅜	10	1.0	4	10.0	15	38.0	28	71.0	41	104.0
½	13	1.3	4½	11.5	16	40.5	29	73.5	42	106.5
⅝	15	1.5	5	12.5	17	43.0	30	76.0	43	109.0
¾	20	2.0	5½	14	18	46.0	31	79.0	44	112.0
⅞	22	2.2	6	15.0	19	48.5	32	81.5	45	114.5
1	25	2.5	7	18.0	20	51.0	33	84.0	46	117.0
1¼	32	3.8	8	20.5	21	53.5	34	86.5	47	119.5
1½	38	3.8	9	23.0	22	56.0	35	89.0	48	122.0
1¾	45	4.5	10	25.5	23	58.5	36	91.5	49	124.5
2	50	5.0	11	28.0	24	61.0	37	94.0	50	127.0
2½	65	6.5	12	30.5	25	63.5	38	96.5		

Skill Levels

Beginner projects for first-time knitters using basic stitches. Minimal shaping.

Easy projects using basic stitches, repetitive stitch patterns, simple color changes, and simple shaping and finishing.

Intermediate projects with a variety of stitches, mid-level shaping and finishing.

Experienced projects using advanced techniques and stitches, detailed shaping and refined finishing.

E-mail: Customer_Service@whitebirches.com

HOUSE of WHITE BIRCHES
PUBLISHERS SINCE 1947

Easy Turtleback Jackets is published by DRG, 306 East Parr Road, Berne, IN 46711, telephone (260) 589-4000. Printed in USA. Copyright © 2009 DRG. All rights reserved. This publication may not be reproduced in part or in whole without written permission from the publisher.

RETAIL STORES: If you would like to carry this pattern book or any other DRG publications, call the Wholesale Department at Annie's Attic to set up a direct account: (903) 636-4303. Also, request a complete listing of publications available from DRG.

Every effort has been made to ensure that the instructions in this pattern book are complete and accurate. We cannot, however, take responsibility for human error, typographical mistakes or variations in individual work.

STAFF

Editor: Jeanne Stauffer
Assistant Editor: Erika Mann
Technical Editor: Kathy Wesley
Technical Artist: Nicole Gage
Copy Supervisor: Michelle Beck
Copy Editor: Amanda Ladig
Graphic Arts Supervisor: Ronda Bechinski

Graphic Artists: Erin Augsburger, Debby Keel
Art Director: Brad Snow
Assistant Art Director: Nick Pierce
Photography Supervisor: Tammy Christian
Photography: Matt Owen
Photo Stylist: Tammy Steiner

ISBN: 978-1-59217-271-9

1 2 3 4 5 6 7 8 9

House of White Birches, Berne, Indiana 46711   DRGnetwork.com

Photo Index

6

10

4

8

12

16

14

18